D1533199

TIME TRAVELING TO

1953

CELEBRATING A SPECIAL YEAR

TIME TRAVELING TO 1953

Author
Edward L. Jones

Design
Gonçalo Sousa

November 2022
ISBN: 9798363192937

Surprise!

Dear reader, thank you so much for purchasing my book!

To make this book more (much more!) affordable, the images are all black & white, but I've created a special gift for you!

You can now have access, for FREE, to the PDF version of this book with the original images!

Keep in mind that some are originally black & white, but a lot of them are colored.

Go to page 99 and follow the instructions to download it.

I hope you enjoy it!

Contents

Chapter I: News & Current Events 1953

Leading Events

January 20th: Inauguration Of Dwight D. Eisenhower

President Dwight D. Eisenhower giving a speech

Dwight David "Ike" Eisenhower was born in Denison, Texas, on October 14th, 1890. He decided to run for President in 1952 and won the ballot to be the Republican Candidate, with California Senator Richard M. Nixon running as his Vice President. The election took place on November 4th, 1952, between Eisenhower and the Democratic Party candidate Adlai E. Stevenson. Eisenhower won an overwhelming 39 states (442 electoral votes) to Stevenson's 9 states (89 electoral votes) (britannica.com). Eisenhower was sworn in as the 34th President of The United States on January 20th. Some of the key milestones of his first term in office were the expansion of the social security system, an increase in the minimum wage that reached $1 an hour, the creation of the Department of Health, Education, and Welfare, the

President Dwight D. Eisenhower signing the Civil Rights Act (H.R. 6127)

Richard M. Nixon

Dwight D. Eisenhower and Richard M. Nixon
at the Republican convention

Dwight D. Eisenhower with running mate Richard Nixon

expiration of controls that covered rent, wages, and prices, plus the handing over of tideland oil reserves to the individual states. On the international front, Eisenhower was responsible for the truce/end of the Korean War in 1953, and the eventual establishment of the International Atomic Energy Agency in 1957. His use of covert operations to overthrow governments in Iran and Guatemala would be viewed less positively in later years. Despite a heart attack in 1955, Eisenhower ran for a second term (with Nixon) and again beat Stevenson in November 1956. Dwight D. Eisenhower died on March 28th, 1969.

January 31st-February 1st: North Sea Flood

One of the 20th century's worst peacetime disasters unfolded at the end of January 1953. The massive storm that resulted from a combination of annual spring tides and a deep pressure system. This included intense, gale force winds that caused widespread flooding in Holland, Belgium,

The tremendous damage brought by the flood to the Dutch islands

Scotland, and England. The situation was worsened by the enclosed landscape and shallowness of the North Sea, and the narrow entrance to the English Channel at the southern point. Wind speeds were recorded at 126mph (203kmh), and the peak of the surge may have been anything between 3.35 to 5.6 meters above average sea level. Waves of nearly 5 meters were also reported. The first casualty of the environmental disaster was the M.V. Princess Victoria passenger ferry. She set off as usual from Stranraer in Scotland, but sank a couple of hours later due to the storm. Of the 179 passengers and crew, 133 died and

In Nieuwerkerk in Duiveland

only 44 survived. The damage and destruction caused by the event was huge. In England alone, 140,000 acres were flooded, 24,000 properties damaged, 46,000 livestock killed, and 307 people lost their lives. In Holland, it was even worse. 340,000 acres were flooded, 47,300 buildings damaged and 1,836 lives lost. Elsewhere, 39 people died in Belgium and Scotland, and 230 were lost at sea (of which the Princess Victoria accounted for 133).

March 5th: The Death Of Joseph Stalin

Joseph Stalin

Iosif/Josef Vissarionovich Djugashvili/Dzhugashvili (Joseph Stalin) was born on December 18th, 1878 (December 6th in the old-style calendar), in Gori, Georgia. He became Secretary-General of the Soviet Union Communist Party in 1922, and was the Soviet Union's Premier between 1941 and his death in 1953. On the evening of February 28th, Stalin gathered his inner circle of close associates - Georgy Malenkov, Lavrenti (Lavrety) Beria, Nikita Khrushchev, and Nikolai Bulganin - to watch a film and have some drinks at his Kuntsevo dacha near Moscow. The convivial meeting continued until the early hours of the morning when the quartet left. Stalin was

Joseph Stalin and Nikita Khrushchev having a meeting

found late the next day, lying on the floor in his pajamas; the reports of whether he was totally unconscious or barely coherent vary. Doctors eventually diagnosed a massive stroke, although there remains speculation that he may have been poisoned by something like warfarin, and at 21:50 on March 5th, he was pronounced dead. His body was embalmed and placed with Lenin's in the Lenin-Stalin Mausoleum. Stalin was initially succeeded by Malenkov for six months before he was forced to resign and Khrushchev took over. In October 1961, Stalin's body was removed from the mausoleum and buried by the Kremlin Wall.

Joseph Stalin, portrait photograph, side view

May 29th: Sir Edmund Hillary And Tenzing Norgay Conquer Mount Everest

During May 1953, New Zealand's Edmund Hillary and Nepal Sherpa Tenzing Norgay became the first two men to climb up to the summit of Mount Everest, the highest point on Earth at 29,035 feet above sea level. Hillary and Norgay were part of a 14-member group that attempted to reach the summit. Hillary, Norgay, and three others made camp at 27,900 feet on May 28th, and the next morning, Hillary and Norgay set out to reach the top of the world; at 11:30 on May 29th, the two men achieved their monumental objective.

Edmund Hillary and Tenzing Norgay after reaching the Mount Everest summit

They stayed there for 15 minutes, during which Hillary took the iconic pictures that became known around the world. While at the summit, Hillary also left a crucifix, and Norgay some sweets and biscuits as a Buddhist offering (history.com).

June 2nd: Coronation Of H.R.H. Queen Elizabeth II

Queen Elizabeth II Coronation Souvenir

Princess Elizabeth Alexandra Mary, who later became H.R.H. Queen Elizabeth II, was born on April 21st, 1926, and was the daughter of King George VI (previously known as Prince Albert, Duke of York) and Queen Elizabeth (previously known as Lady Elizabeth Bowes Lyon, and who later became known as the Queen Mother). It had never been expected that Princess Elizabeth would be Queen, at least not in her early years. Her father was the younger son of King George V, but when King Edward VIII abdicated by choice on December 10th, 1936 (so he could marry Wallis Simpson, a divorced American woman), her father unexpectedly ascended to the throne. During the latter stage of World War II (1945), Princess Elizabeth trained to become a driver and mechanic as part of the Auxiliary Territorial Service. Just after the war, she married Lieutenant Philip Mountbatten (previously known as Prince Philip of Greece and Denmark) on November 20th, 1947, at Westminster Abbey. Princess Elizabeth began to take on more of her father's duties during 1951 due to his failing health. During the journey to Australia and New Zealand for a royal tour (with Prince Philip), the Princess was informed that King George VI had died on February 6th, 1952.

She carried out the first opening of Parliament as the new Queen on November 4th, 1952, and her official coronation was scheduled for June 2nd, 1953, at Westminster Abbey. The ceremony was conducted by Geoffrey Francis Fisher, the Archbishop of Canterbury, and it was the first (and still) only coronation to be broadcast live on television. The young Queen had been advised by many senior figures, including the Archbishop, Prime Minister Winston Churchill, and members of the cabinet, to not have the

Elizabeth II wearing the Imperial State Crown and holding the Sovereign's Sceptre and Orb

event televised, but the new Queen was steadfast and refused to change her mind; she wanted the people to be able to witness and participate in her coronation. It is thought that less than two million homes had a television at the start of 1953, but in the week preceding the coronation, an estimated 526,000 televisions were sold. Various figures have been given for that momentous day; it is estimated that 20 million people watched the service on television in the U.K., including 10.4 million who watched it on television at the home of friends or family, plus a

Elizabeth II on the Royal Tour of New Zealand

further 1.5 million who viewed it in pubs and cinemas (bbc.com). It was the first event where the viewing figures surpassed those of radio listeners. The BBC coverage, with commentary for the actual service delivered by Richard Dimbleby, was broadcast around the world, including 85 million who watched it in the United States. H.R.H. Queen Elizabeth II has since gone on to become the longest-reigning British Monarch. At the age of 95, she is still the Queen of The United Kingdom and the Commonwealth.

July 27th: The End Of The Korean War

The Korean War originally started on June 25th, 1950, when troops from the North Korean army crossed over the boundary that separated the northern, Soviet-supported Democratic People's Republic of Korea and the southern, western-nation backed Republic of Korea. Although peace talks started in July 1951, the Korean War would rage on for two more years. Peace negotiations began again on April 26th, 1953, and despite fierce last-minute fighting, an Armistice was signed on July 27th by the United States, China, and Korea. It consisted of something like the original pre-war border along the 38th parallel, although it did give South Korea an extra 1,500 square miles of territory, with the creation of a demilitarized zone about 2 miles wide that is still in operation today. South Korean President Syngman Rhee accepted the agreement, but South Korea did not sign it at the time. This meant the Korean War officially continued, and still does with the

Korean girl with her brother trudges by a stalled M-26 tank

absence of an official peace treaty/declaration. The three years of actual fighting claimed the lives of around 5 million people. About half of those were civilians, while 40,000 American soldiers were killed (plus 100,000 were wounded) along with 46,000 South Koreans. It has been estimated that 215,000 North Koreans were killed along with 400,000 Chinese (nationalgeographic.com).

Other Major Events

October 6th: Fidel Castro Sentenced To 15 Years

Fidel Alejandro Castro Ruz was born on August 13th, 1926, in Cuba. In June 1952, Cuba was supposed to hold elections, but they never took place. They were canceled when President Carlos Prío Socarrás' government was overthrown in a bloodless military coup d'état on March 10th by General Fulgencio Batista, the former President who ruled Cuba between 1933 and 1944. There were attempts to remove Batista by legal means, but these failed, so Castro attempted to remove him by force on July 26th, 1953. In the early hours of that

Fidel Castro

morning, Castro attacked a base that housed Batista's troops, the Moncada Barracks in Santiago. He led a group of around 150 supporters, who were armed with only .22 caliber rifles and a few other weapons. Castro's forces were outgunned and out-manned, and the audacious assault that was intended to inspire a revolution failed. There are numerous reports that state different casualty figures. Some say the majority were killed, while another gives actual figures of 8 killed, 11 injured, and 70 taken prisoner (PBS.

org). What is not disputed is the fact that Castro and his brother, Raúl Castro, were eventually caught and placed in prison themselves. At a trial on October 16th, 1953, Castro was jailed for 15 years, but both he and his brother were released on May 15th, 1955, in a political prisoner amnesty. In February 1959, he became Cuban Prime Minister.

November 20-22: Operation Castor At Điên Biên Phu

French paratrooper operating his automatic weapon during "Operation Castor"

France's Operation Castor was the largest airborne operation that had been instigated since World War II. It began on November 20th when French forces landed in Điên Biên Phu in northwest Vietnam with the intention of taking the old airstrip that had been originally built by Japan when they occupied Vietnam during W.W.II. The French invasion force consisted of five to six battalions and were commanded by Brigadier General Jean Gilles.

Throughout the next two days, over 4,000 French soldiers landed in Điên Biên Phu, but during their arrival, the French troops unexpectedly ran into a regiment of the Viet Minh army who were on field exercise.

Paratroopers of the French-Indochinese Union army

A small battle erupted between the two sides, which cost 16 French lives (47 wounded) and 115 Viet Minh casualties (4 wounded) (academic.com). The operation was generally considered successful, but a much bigger conflict would soon erupt; The Battle Of Điên Biên Phu in 1954 could be considered the precursor of the Vietnam War that would rage for the next twenty years.

December 30th: First Color Televisions Go On Sale In The United States

On December 17th, the Federal Communications Commission in the United States approved a recommendation from the National Television System Committee regarding the RCA Sequential color system. It was the intention of RCA to broadcast the New Year's Day Rose Parade in color to select markets, including Los Angeles, San Francisco, Denver, Chicago, Washington, and New York. Very soon after the approval, on December 30th, the first color television sets went on sale. Two models were released that day: the

The first color TV that went on sale

RCA CT-100 and the Admiral C1617A which were both 15-inch screens. They were remarkably expensive. The CT-100 cost around $1,000-$1,175 in early 1954 - that's over $10,000 dollars today (April 2022).

Political Events

August 12th: First Thermonuclear Test By The Soviet Union

On August 12th, the Soviet Union tested its first thermonuclear device. The test took place at the Semipalatinsk site, which was located in northern Kazakhstan, and it involved the Joe-4 bomb. The bomb featured

First test at Semipalatinsk, Kazakhstan

a layer cake design that comprised both uranium and hydrogen in alternative layers, and the blast yield was around 400 kilotons. Although that was a lot larger than the bomb dropped on Hiroshima, it was considerably less than a device tested by the Americans several months earlier. The Soviets argued that while it lagged behind in terms of power, it was small enough to be delivered from an airplane.

August 19th: Elected Prime Minister Of Iran Overthrown In A Coup

Both the United States and United Kingdom, and more specifically the Central Intelligence Agency and M.I.6, were involved in the military coup d'état that overthrew the established Iranian government on August 19th. Mohammad Mossadegh/Mosaddegh had become a powerful figure in Iranian politics, and on April 28th, Shah Mohammad Reza Shah Pahlavi was effectively forced to appoint Mossadegh as Iranian Prime Minister due to his popularity and a 79-12 vote by the Majlis. His oil nationalization plans caused friction within both Iran and the wider world, especially those in the West. Britain withdrew from the Iranian oil market,

Mohammad Mosaddegh

and there were fears in America that the Soviet Union could potentially seize control of the government. The Americans were initially resistant to the idea of overthrowing Mossadegh and the Iranian government, but with persuasion from Britain and a reluctant agreement from the Shah, Operation Ajax was formed. The C.I.A. and M.I.6 worked together and provided financial assistance to the Iranian military, and on August 19th, the coup was initiated. Mossadegh was removed from power. General Fazallah/Fazlollah Zahedi was picked as the man to lead Iran after the coup, while Mossadegh was jailed for three years on treason charges. After this, he was placed indefinitely on house arrest until his death on March 5th, 1967.

Other Notable Events

January 14th First Robertson Panel Meeting into U.F.O.s

In early 1953, Dr. H. Marshall Chadwell (the Assistant Director for the Office of Scientific Investigations) and Dr. H.P. Robertson (a respected California Institute Of Technology physicist) were tasked with bringing together a panel of distinguished, reputable, and notable scientists to investigate the issue of Unidentified Flying Objects. The group comprised Dr. Samuel A. Goudsmit (nuclear physicist: Brookhaven National Laboratories), Dr. Luis W. Alvarez (high-energy physicist), Dr. Thornton Page (Deputy Director: John

Luiz Alvarez

Hopkins Operations Research Office, plus radar and electronics expert), and Dr. Lloyd V. Berkner (Director: Brookhaven National Laboratories, plus an expert in geophysics). Between 14th-18th January, the panel convened to scientifically appraise if there were any potential dangers to U.S. security from the U.F.O. phenomena. Having looked at all the data and evidence, the panel agreed that there were reasonable explanations for almost all, if not entirely all, of the recorded sightings. Their conclusion stated that there was no threat to national security based on the U.F.O. evidence they had been given.

March 17th Operation Upshot-Knothole

The United States conducted a series of nuclear tests in Nevada between March and June, and eleven test shots in total were conducted during the operation. Around 21,000 military personnel took part in the ground exercise called Desert Rock V that was connected with the Grable test. In an attempt by the U.S. government and military to lessen public fears over nuclear weapons, the first test on March 17th was conducted in public - it was called an "Open Shot" - and it was witnessed by reporters. The initial test, nicknamed Annie, was an experimental device that was code-named

GRABLE Event - The First Atomic Cannon

Upshot-Knothole GRABLE, 1953

XR3. Ten more tests took place on 03/24, 03/31, 04/06, 04/11, 04/18, 04/25, 05/08, 05/19, 03/25, and 06/04. The test called Climax on June 4th very much lived up to its name; it was the biggest explosion of the operation with a yield of 61 kilotons. However, it was the test on May 25th (Grable) that was most significant because it was the first test of a nuclear artillery shell that was fired from a 280mm cannon called Atomic Annie.

March 26th: Medical Researcher Jonas Salk Successfully Tests Polio Vaccine

Dr. Jonas Edward Salk

Administration of the polio inoculation at the University of Pittsburgh

Dr. Jonas Salk was a medical researcher from the University of Pittsburgh, and he announced on March 26th, via C.B.S. national radio, that he had successfully tested the world's first polio vaccine in preliminary trials. The disease had been in the news just the previous year because of a polio epidemic in 1952. Figures for 1952 recorded that there were 58,000 cases of polio and over 3,000 people died from it (history.com). Salk had been so confident about his experimental vaccine that he gave it to his son, Peter Salk, his wife, his two other sons, and himself on March 16th. The vaccine was officially declared safe in April 1955, and a massive campaign to inoculate people was instigated. Despite a setback when 200,000 people were injected with a faulty vaccine, cases of polio dropped to less than 6,000 within four years (history.com). In honor of his achievement, Salk was given the Presidential Medal of Freedom in 1977.

June 7th-9th: Flint-Worcester Tornado Outbreak

The newspaper headlines

During June 1953, a series of tornados wreaked havoc across Kansas, Colorado, Nebraska, South Dakota, Iowa, Minnesota, Montana, Ohio, Michigan, Massachusetts, and New Hampshire. A total of 50 tornadoes swept across the aforementioned parts of America between June 7th and June 9th. The first in the sequence appeared around 19:00 on June 7th with three tornadoes from the same squall line that hit Graham County in Kansas. They were fairly mild compared to what would follow over the next few days. A further 22 were recorded up to 23:45, with another 11 counted prior to 05:00 the next morning. The worst of those was a Force 4 that hit Sherman/Valley counties around 21:15. It killed 11 people and caused $500,000 of damage. The weather returned with a vengeance around 22:00 on June 8th, with the first

A path of absolute devastation

tornado hitting Deuel County. Eleven more events were recorded that night. The worst tornado on that day was the lone Force 5 of the period that touched down in Flint and Beecher (Michigan); it caused 116 fatalities and injured 844

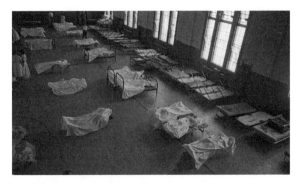

The National Guard armory, turned into a makeshift morgue

people, and is still ranked as the 10th deadliest tornado in American history (Statista-2019). A Force 4 in Monroe, Michigan, killed 4, and another in northeast Ohio killed 17 people. On the evening of June 9th, just when everyone probably thought it was over, another four tornadoes appeared across Massachusetts and New Hampshire. The first was a Force 4 that struck Worcester County in Massachusetts - 94 people were killed and 1,228 people were injured (it was the most people killed on record by a Force 4 tornado). The last to appear was a Force 1 in Strafford County, New Hampshire. Overall, 247 died, 2,562 people were injured, and it caused $340.6 million of damage, a figure equal to $3.28 billion in 2021 (wordisk. com/academic.com).

November 20th: Piltdown Man Discovery in 1912 Proved To Be A Hoax

One of the greatest scientific hoaxes was confirmed in 1953 when it was proved that the Piltdown Man discovery was a forgery. In 1912, Charles Dawson, an amateur archeologist, contacted the Natural History Museum in London, claiming to have found the missing link between apes and humans. The "discovery" also involved Arthur Smith Woodward, a paleontologist. Dawson presented pieces of a skull and an ape-like jawbone (plus other items such as stone tools and fossil fragments). The 'missing link' was scientifically named Eoanthropus Dawsoni. Dawson claimed the skull pieces were found in gravel beds he'd excavated in Piltdown, Sussex. As more historic finds were unearthed during the 1920s and 1930s, it became obvious they bore little resemblance to the Piltdown Man. Three scientists from Oxford (Joseph Weiner, Kenneth Oakley, and Wilfred Le Gros Park) conducted a series of tests on the Piltdown Man fragments, and unveiled their findings in Time Magazine in November 1953. It was proved that the skull fragments were nowhere near as old as had been claimed. Later investigations proved that the jawbone was from an orangutan subspecies, while the human evidence was from two or more human specimens. Many culprits have been suggested, some just accomplices, but the majority of investigators consider that Dawson alone was probably responsible for the hoax.

"The Fossil Man of Sussex," news of the "discovery"

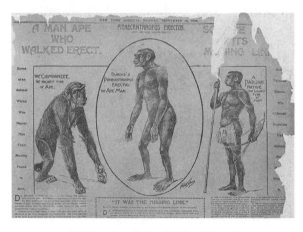

"A Man Ape Who Walked Erect,"
New York Journal

Chapter II: Crime & Punishment 1953

Major Crime Events

January 19th-July 15th: British Serial Killer John Christie Murders Final Three Victims

John Christie

John Reginald Halliday Christie was a British serial killer who was responsible for at least six (maybe eight) murders between 1943 and 1953. His murder spree began during August 1943 when he strangled Ruth Fuerst during sex and buried her in the communal garden at 10 Rillington Place. Christie struck again the next year on October 21st, 1944, when he promised to cure Muriel Amelia Eady's bronchitis by using a gas he'd concocted. Instead, the gas knocked her out; he then choked her to death and raped her postmortem.

He buried her body in the same garden. It is not known for sure whether Christie killed his neighbors, Beryl and Geraldine Evans (the latter being a 15-month-old child). One theory is that Christie again used gas to render Beryl unconscious, strangled her, and raped her. He may have killed the child afterward. Other hypotheses suggest it was Timothy Evans who killed his wife and child. Timothy Evans confessed, then withdrew his confession, and was tried, found guilty of both murders (with evidence from Christie), and hanged on March 9th, 1950. His conviction for the murder of Geraldine

Evans was posthumously pardoned (but not declared innocent) in 1966. Christie had admitted killing Beryl but not Geraldine. The likelihood is that Timothy Evans was completely innocent, but the definitive truth will never be known.

Christie went on to kill his own wife by strangulation (December 12th, 1952), who he claimed had gone back to Sheffield, and hid her body under floorboards. Between January 19th and March 6th, Christie killed Rita Nelson (January 19th), Kathleen Maloney (February 25th), and Hectorina McLennan (March 6th - different reports state her surname was MacLennan and even McLennon), and all of them were suspected of being gassed, strangled, and raped. Their bodies were hidden in an alcove behind a kitchen cupboard that Christie concealed by papering over it. He tried to hide the smell by using disinfectant, and on March 20th, rented the apartment to another family and left. It was illegal to do this and the landlord asked them to leave within days. The bodies were found during renovations to the kitchen and the police were called. During a search, the body of Ethel Christie was found under the floor, plus the bodies of Fuerst and Eady in the garden. The police launched a manhunt and Christie was arrested on March 31st. The statements he gave were full of discrepancies and lies, and even justifications such as mercy killings for some of his actions (this also raises some debate about the order of the killings). His trial began on June 22nd for the murder of his wife, and despite the defense claiming he was not guilty due to insanity, Christie was convicted of murder four days later. His death sentence was carried out on July 15th when he was hanged at Pentonville Prison.

June 19th: Julius and Ethel Rosenberg Executed For Spying

Julius and Ethel Rosenberg were two New Yorkers born between September 1915 (Ethel) and May 1918 (Julius). Julius was a U.S. Army Signal Corps civilian engineer and Ethel was a clerk. They were married in 1939 and had

Julius and Ethel Rosenberg during their trial for espionage

two sons. They both became members of the Communist Party of the United States of America. On June 17th, 1950, Julius Rosenberg was arrested for espionage and spying, and his wife was arrested a couple of months later. The case against them was based upon evidence that Ethel Rosenberg's brother, Sergeant David Greenglass, had passed data regarding nuclear weapons to the Rosenbergs (information which he had obtained while working on the Manhattan Project), and they, in turn, handed the information to Harry Gold (a spy ring courier). Gold then gave the information to Anatoly A. Yakovlev (the Soviet Union Vice Consul). Gold had been arrested earlier in the year because of his connection with the British spy, Klaus Fuchs. The Rosenbergs' trial began on March 6th, 1951, and despite maintaining they were innocent, they were sentenced to death on April 5th, 1951. Both Julius and Ethel Rosenberg were executed by electric chair on June 19th. The execution made news itself due to Ethel being removed from the chair after three shocks, only for officials to realize that her heart was still beating. They had to

News of the execution

put her back in the chair and two more shocks were applied, these proving fatal. Greenglass was given a 15-year jail term and eventually served around nine years.

September 28th: Bobby Greenlease Kidnapping And Murder

Carl Austin Hall and Bonnie Heady

Robert Cosgrove Greenlease, Jr. was the six-year-old son of Virginia Greenlease and Robert Cosgrove Greenlease, Sr., a multi-millionaire Cadillac dealer who lived in Mission Hills, Kansas. Bobby Greenlease attended the French Institute of Notre Dame de Sion Catholic School in Kansas City. On September 28th, a woman claiming to be Bobby's aunt came to the school to say that his mother had suffered a heart attack and been taken to hospital. She claimed his mother had asked for him and she would take him there. Reports state the youngster even took the woman's hand as if he actually knew her. Later that day, the Greenlease family received a ransom note demanding $600,000 for the return of their son. It was the first of many letters and calls. The family paid the ransom money about a week after the abduction (on the second attempt); it was the largest ransom ever paid at the time. The kidnappers told Bobby's parents on October 5th that they had the money and that he would be returned in 24 hours. What his parents didn't know was that the kidnappers - Carl Austin Hall and Bonnie Emily Heady - had already killed Bobby Greenlease in a field about 30 minutes after he was abducted. Hall tried to strangle him and eventually shot him in the head with a .38 pistol. Hall and Heady went to St.

Louis, and on October 5th, Hall abandoned Heady and took off with all but $2,000 of the money. Hall was arrested on 6th October thanks to a tip-off from a cab driver, and he told them where to find Heady. The body of Bobby Greenlease, Jr. was found buried near the Heady residence in St. Joseph, Missouri. Both Hall and Heady were found guilty and sentenced to the death penalty. On December 18th, Hall and Heady were executed together by lethal gas at the State Penitentiary in Jefferson City.

Other Crime Related Events

January 9th: The Last Woman Hanged In Canada

Marguerite Pitre

Marguerite Pitre was convicted of being an accomplice in the bombing of Canadian Pacific Airlines Flight 108 on September 9th, 1949. The attack killed 23 people. Joseph-Albert Guay was found guilty of planning the bombing; it had been set up to kill his wife, Rita Guay. He was executed (hanged) on January 12th, 1951. During the investigation, he incriminated Généreux Ruest; she had designed and built the bomb. He also accused Marguerite Pitre (Ruest's sister), saying she had delivered it to Canada Airlines to be transferred onto the flight. Ruest was hanged on July 25th, 1952, and Pitre was hanged on January 9th, 1953; she was the 13th and last woman to be executed in Canada.

May 31st: Towpath Murders In Britain

With the United Kingdom preparing for the coronation of H.R.H. Queen Elizabeth II, Barbara Songhurst (aged 16) and Christine Reed (aged 18) were attacked and murdered on May 31st. The two girls had been seen around 23:00 as they rode along the towpath near Teddington Lock in

"Daily Express" newspaper

Middlesex and again at around 23:30. The girls never returned home and the police were called in. Songhurst's body was found the next day, two miles downriver after a crime scene with a trail of blood led to the water where the body had been dumped. She had a fractured skull, stab wounds, and had been raped. Reed's body was found near Glover's Island on June 6th with similar wounds (stabbed six times), and she had also been sexually assaulted. The break came on June 28th when a motorist gave a hitchhiker a lift, and the passenger reminded the driver of the mystery man who was wanted for a rape in Oxshott Heath a week before Songhurst and Reed were murdered. He reported it to the police, and they arrested Alfred Charles Whiteway that day. The key evidence was blood on Whiteway's shoes, his ability to throw a knife (an explanation of how he overpowered two girls at once), and a hatchet (with traces of blood according to some reports) that had previously been lost (which is a story of its own, but was re-found being used by an officer at home). Whiteway was convicted on November 2nd. An appeal was rejected on December 7th, and Whiteway was hanged at Wandsworth Prison on December 22nd.

September 25th: Special Agent John Brady Murphy Mortally Wounded In Gunfight

Special Agent John Brady Murphy was killed by John Elgin Johnson after being involved in a gunfight with the career criminal. Johnson was given a 15-year sentence in 1940 for bank robberies, and after an escape attempt from Leavenworth, he was incarcerated on Alcatraz in 1944 until his

 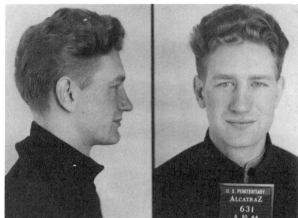

Special Agent J. Brady Murphy   John Elgin Johnson

release in 1953. He became a suspect when a new friend of his was found murdered, and the F.B.I. began a search for Johnson. He was tracked down when he made a telephone call to a Los Angeles reporter from a Baltimore cinema/movie theater. The call was traced, and when four agents attempted to apprehend Johnson, he opened fire. Johnson was shot and killed, but two of the agents were also shot, including Murphy, who was shot in the abdomen. Special Agent Murphy died the next day, on September 26th.

Chapter III: Entertainment 1953

Silver Screen

The world of entertainment in 1953 was quite dissimilar to what modern audiences experience. Television was still in its infancy, CDs and the modern musical production techniques that are taken for granted nowadays were still decades away, and many films in the cinema were still made in black and white. Although there were films made in color as far back as the 1920s and several noteworthy color movies in the 1930s and 1940s, the wholesale change to color would make significant progress in the following 5-10 years.

Cyd Charisse

Disney's Peter Pan,
original magazine ad

Peter Pan

The top-grossing movie of 1953 was actually an animated film - Disney's 'Peter Pan'. It was made in color and released on February 5th. The movie featured the voices of Bobby Driscoll (Peter), Kathryn Beaumont (Wendy Darling), Hans Conried (George Darling/Captain Hook), and Tom Conway (narrator). Box office records dating back to the fifties are far from reliable, but based on figures from the-numbers.com, 'Peter Pan' grossed over $60 million in 1953 and has since gone on to top over $87 million overall. It nearly doubled the figure of the second most successful film in 1953.

Remaining Top Three Films 1953

Finishing second in 1953 was 'The Robe', a Historical/Biblical epic that told a fictional dramatic story around the crucifixion of Jesus Christ. The film starred the enigmatic Richard Burton (Marcellus Gallio) and Jean Simons (Diana) and was directed by Henry Koster. It was the first movie to be filmed in CinemaScope and it grossed $36 million. Claiming the third spot in 1953 was 'From Here To Eternity', a Drama film based around the lives of U.S. soldiers in Hawaii during the few months prior to the 1941 Pearl Harbor attack. The

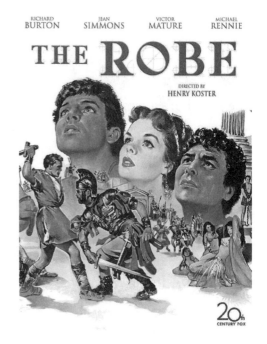

The Robe

film featured several Hollywood stars such as Montgomery Clift (Robert E. Lee Prewitt), Burt Lancaster (Sgt. Milton Warden), Deborah Kerr (Karen Holmes), Frank Sinatra (Angelo Maggio), and Ernest Borgnine (Sgt. "Fatso" Judson). The film grossed over $30 million and won eight Oscars, including Best Picture, Best Supporting Actor (Sinatra), Best Supporting Actress (Kerr), and Best Director (Fred Zinnemann).

Deborah Kerr & Burt Lancaster, 1953

Other Top Ten Films 1953

House of Wax

Even in 1953, there was still a place for Horror films, and the fourth most successful movie of that year was 'House of Wax'. The story centered on a sculptor who makes wax models, but his work is destroyed in a fire started by his business partner. Believed to be dead, he eventually returns and makes new wax sculptors, this time using murdered people. The film starred Vincent Price (Professor Henry Jarrod), Frank Lovejoy (Det. Lt. Tom Brennan), Phyllis Kirk (Sue Allen), and an early role for Charles Bronson (Igor). A top film that year at the box office, it was also the first color 3-D movie. 'Shane' was another film that would go on to be remembered by many and watched by countless people over the years. The film was about a gunfighter who decides to look for a quieter life and becomes friends with a family who own a homestead. He eventually helps them to fight against cattle barons who are intimidating them. It starred Alan Ladd (Shane), Jean Arthur (Marian Starrett), Jack Palance (Jack Wilson), and Emile Meyer (Rufus

Shane

Gentlemen Prefer Blondes

Ryker). Whether someone is a film fan or not, the vast majority of people will have heard of 'Gentlemen Prefer Blondes'. The Musical Comedy focused on two showgirls working on a cruise ship headed to Paris, where one of them intends to get married. The film starred Jane Russell (Dorothy Shaw), Marilyn Monroe (Lorelei Lee), and Charles Coburn (Sir Francis Beekman). The movie is often remembered for the song 'Diamonds Are a Girl's Best Friend', sung by Monroe.

'Diamonds Are a Girl's Best Friend' album cover

🎬 Box Office Figures 1953

the-numbers.com: Top Grossing Movies of 1953 At The Domestic Box Office

Rank	Title	Total Gross
1	Peter Pan	$60,087,855
2	The Robe	$36,000,000
3	From Here to Eternity	$30,481,824
4	House Of Wax	$23,800,000
5	Shane	$20,000,000
6	Gentlemen Prefer Blondes	$12,000,000
7	Hondo	$,8,200,000
8	How to Marry a Millionaire	$7,300,000
9	The Beast From 20,000 Fathoms	$5,000,000
10	Niagara	$2,500,000

Other Film Releases

There were a few other films in 1953 that didn't make the Top Ten but which may be familiar to many movie enthusiasts today. 'The War of the Worlds', starring Gene Barry (Dr. Clayton Forrester) and Ann Robinson (Sylvia van Buren), was released on August 13th, and it was the first cinematic version (in color) that retold the famous novel of the same name by H.G. Wells.

The War of the Worlds

Calamity Jane   Kiss Me Kate

'Calamity Jane', a Musical Western featuring Doris Day (Calamity Jane) and Howard Keel (Wild Bill Hickok), was another movie with a title that many people will have heard of, even if they haven't seen the movie. Keel would appear in a second movie during 1953 that is probably equally known to people just from the title.

'Kiss Me Kate' was a Hollywood version of the Broadway Musical that shared the same name. It featured Kathryn Grayson (Lilli Vanessi/ Katherine), Keel (Fred Graham/Petruchio), and Ann Miller (Lois Lane/ Bianca).

Award Winners 1953

The 10th Golden Globe Awards - Thursday, February 26th, 1953: Ambassador Hotel, Hotel, Los Angeles, CA.

🏆 Winners

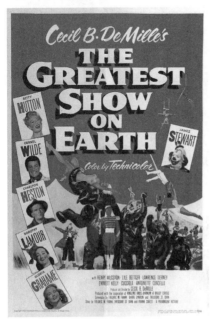

Best Motion Picture Drama
- The Greatest Show On Earth

Best Motion Picture Musical/Comedy -
With A Song in My Heart

Best Actress Motion Picture Drama - Shirley
Booth (Come Back, Little Sheba)

Best Actor Motion Picture Drama -
Gary Cooper (High Noon)

Best Actress Motion Picture Musical/
Comedy - Susan Hayward (With A Song
In My Heart)

Best Actor Motion Picture Musical/
Comedy - Donald O'Connor (Singin' In
The Rain)

Best Supporting Actress Motion Picture -
Katy Jurado (High Noon)

Best Supporting Actor Motion Picture -
Millard Mitchell (My Six Convicts)

Best Director Motion Picture - Cecil B.
DeMille (The Greatest Show On Earth)

The 6th British Academy Of Film And Television Arts Awards - Thursday, March 5th, 1953: Leicester Square Theatre, London.

🏆 **Winners**

Best British Film - The Sound Barrier

Best British Actor (Film) - Ralph Richardson (The Sound Barrier)

Best British Actress (Film) - Vivien Leigh (A Streetcar Named Desire)

Best Foreign Actor (Film) - Marlon Brando (Viva, Zapata!)

Best Foreign Actress (Film) - Simone Signoret (Casque D'Or/Golden Helmet)

The 25th Academy Awards - Thursday, March 19th, 1953: RKO Pantages Theatre, Hollywood, CA.

The 25th Academy Award winner of Best Picture: The Greatest Show On Earth

♛ Winners

- ☿ Best Actor in a Leading Role - Gary Cooper (High Noon)

- ☿ Best Actor in a Supporting Role - Anthony Quinn (Viva Zapata!)

- ☿ Best Actress in a Leading Role - Shirley Booth (Come Back, Little Sheba)

- ☿ Best Actress in a Supporting Role - Gloria Grahame (The Bad And The Beautiful)

- ☿ Best Director - John Ford (The Quiet Man)

- ☿ Best Music (Music Score Dramatic/Comedy)- High Noon (Dimitri Tiomkin)

- ☿ Best Music (Original Song) - High Noon (Do Not Forsake Me, Oh My Darlin')

- ☿ Best Picture - The Greatest Show On Earth (Cecil B. DeMille)

Top Of The Charts

Best Albums And Singles 1953

There are plenty of lists and ratings pages to show "popular" albums and singles in 1953, but actual sales figures are hard to find and even harder to trust if they can be unearthed. The tracking of physical sales as a mark of an album's success was decades away. The best way to ascertain the best-selling albums and singles worldwide from 1953 is to combine their success and performance across multiple charts. One such website, TSort. info, has compiled a great deal of information on this subject. It provides a comprehensive selection of information from a vast collection of singles and album charts around the world.

While vintage films still retain a decent following with film lovers, it could be argued that music has evolved to such an extent that music from 1953 would be somewhat less familiar to people today than films released in the same year. The top-rated album was 'Music For Lovers Only' by Jackie Gleason, who actually had two entries in the 1953 list. His "mood music" albums proved to be extremely popular, and 'Music For Lovers Only' still held the record for the most weeks in the Billboard Top 10 Albums Chart in 2021 (153).

'Music for Lovers Only' vinyl album cover

Gleason was famous for a number of reasons, ('The Jackie Gleason Show' was a popular TV program in the fifties, as was 'The Honeymooners') but it is likely most people these days will recall him for his utterly outrageous and iconic portrayal of Sheriff Buford T. Justice in the 'Smokey and The Bandit' trilogy - yes, it is the same Jackie Gleason! Other names that will be recognizable several decades later from the Top Ten were Peggy Lee, Mantovani, Thelonious Monk, and Duke Ellington.

Other Albums and Singles

Further down the 1953 album list, the likes of Nat King Cole, Hank Williams, Eartha Kitt, and Marilyn Monroe are still instantly known. A look across the chart for singles provides a few more renowned names and titles, such as Perry Como, Dean Martin, who had a hit in 1953 with 'That's Amore', Tony Bennett,

That's Amore

The Drifters, Frank Sinatra ('I've Got the World On A String'), plus songs like 'Your Cheatin' Heart' (Hank Williams), 'Santa Baby' (Eartha Kitt), and 'How Much Is That Doggy In The Window? (Patti Page and Lita Roza at #26).

I've Got The World On A String

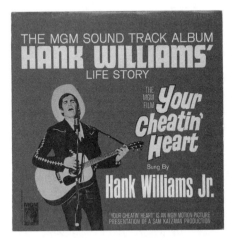

Your Cheatin' Heart

Santa Baby

Lita Roza   Patti Page

Top Albums 1953 (tsort.info):

1. Jackie Gleason - 'Music For Lovers Only'
2. The Quintet - 'Jazz At Massey Hall'
3. Tom Lehrer - 'Songs By Tom Lehrer'
4. Peggy Lee - 'Black Coffee'
5. Mantovani - 'The Music Of Victor Herbert And Sigmund Romberg'
6. Arthur Godfrey - 'Christmas With Arthur Godfrey'
7. Duke Ellington - 'Ellington Uptown'
8. Lennie Tristano - 'Descent Into The Maelstrom'
9. Jackie Gleason - 'Music To Make You Misty'
10. Thelonious Monk - 'Thelonious Monk Trio'

Top Singles 1983 (tsort.info):

1. Les Paul & Mary Ford - 'Vaya Con Dios (May God Be With You)'
2. Perry Como - 'Don't Let The Stars Get In Your Eyes'
3. Percy Faith - 'The Song From Moulin Rouge (Where Is Your Heart)'
4. Eddie Fisher - I'm Walking Behind You'
5. Dean Martin - 'That's Amore'

6. Patti Page - 'How Much Is That Doggy In The Window?'
7. Frankie Laine - 'I Believe'
8. Tony Bennett - 'Rags To Riches'
9. Nat King Cole - 'Pretend'
10. The Ames Brothers - 'You You You'

🏆 Award Winners 1953

Neither the Grammy Awards nor the Brit Awards existed in 1953.

Television

The gulf between television in 1953 and 2022 is every bit as vast as that for film and music. While America already had four main networks even back in 1953, the United Kingdom had just one channel - the BBC. The rules for the BBC back in the 1950s seem rather antiquated when viewed through the prism of modern 24/7, multi-channel, multi-format viewing options. For example, the BBC was only allowed to broadcast between 9am and 11pm, and even then, only two hours of programs were allowed pre-1pm. Possibly the

The "Television Symbol", known informally as the "Bats Wings", was the first BBC Television Service identification

most amazing thing to consider was the fact that there were no television broadcasts between 6-7pm; it was called the "Toddler's Truce" and was designed to allow parents to tell children that programs had finished for the night. Despite this period being nearly seventy years ago at the time of writing, 1953 still had some programs that modern people will have heard of. 'I Love Lucy' is a name that people can easily recall, as is 'Dragnet' and 'You

Bet Your Life' while others that made the Top 30 include 'The Lone Ranger', 'Strike It Rich', 'The Roy Rogers Show', and 'What's My Line?'.

On British television, the choice was a bit limited, and the majority of

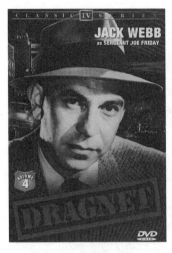

Dragnet, 1951-1959

George Fenneman and
Groucho Marx

Clayton Moore

Strike It Rich

The Roy Rogers Show

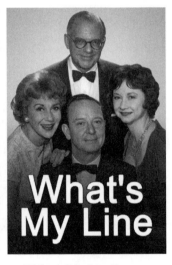

'What's My Line?' poster

programs on the BBC consisted of news-related items and sport. Shows that appeared on British television during 1953 included 'Muffin The Mule', 'Come Dancing', 'Watch with Mother', 'Face The Music', 'Robin Hood',

'The Quatermass Experiment', and the current affairs program 'Panorama', which is still part of the BBC television schedules today.

Panorama

Come Dancing

Muffin the Mule

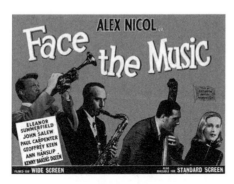

Face the Music

Watch with Mother

'Robin Hood' TV Mini Series

The Quatermass Experiment

📺 Television Ratings 1953 (classic-tv.com)

1952-53 Shows	Est. Audience
1. 'Arthur Godfrey's Talent Scouts'	8,231,400
2. 'Texaco Star Theater'	7,956,000
3. 'I Love Lucy'	7,787,700
4. 'The Red Skelton Show'	7,680,600
5. 'The Colgate Comedy Hour'	6,930,900
6. 'Arthur Godfrey And His Friends'	6,624,900
7. 'Fireside Theatre'	6,594,300
8. 'Your Show Of Shows'	6,579,000
9. 'The Jack Benny Show'	6,548,400
10. 'You Bet Your Life'	6,441,300

1952-53 Shows	Est. Audience
1. 'I Love Lucy'	13,729,200
2. 'Arthur Godfrey's Talent Scouts'	11,158,800
3. 'Arthur Godfrey And His Friends'	9,608,400
4. 'Dragnet'	9,547,200
5. 'Texaco Star Theater'	9,526,800
6. 'The Buick Circus Hour'	9,384,000
7. 'The Colgate Comedy Hour'	9,037,200
8. 'Gangbusters'	8,649,600
9. 'You Bet Your Life'	8,486,400
10. 'Fireside Theatre'	8,282,400

🏆 Award Winners In 1953

In 1953, both the Golden Globe Awards and B.A.F.T.A. Awards only recognized films (the latter was called the British Academy Film Awards in 1953).

The 5th Primetime Emmy Awards - Thursday, February 5th, 1953: Hotel Statler, Los Angeles, CA.

🏆 Winners

- Best Situation Comedy – I Love Lucy

- Best Dramatic Program – Robert Montgomery Presents

- Best Variety Program – Your Show Of Shows

- Best Actor – Thomas Mitchell

- Best Actress – Helen Hayes

- Best Audience Participation, Quiz, or Panel Program – What's My Line?

Desi Arnaz and Lucille Ball

- Best Comedian – Jimmy Durante

- Best Comedienne – Lucille Ball

- Best Mystery, Action, or Adventure Program – Dragnet

Chapter IV: Sports Review 1953

American Sports

December 27th: National Football League Championship Game 1953 (Briggs Stadium)

The N.F.L. was quite different back in 1953. The league consisted of 2 divisions that each had six teams within them. Of the 12 teams, 9 still exist under the same name and city today (Browns, Giants, Eagles, Steelers, Lions, Rams (in Los Angeles), 49ers, Packers, and the Bears). The remaining three were the Chicago Cardinals (now Arizona Cardinals), Washington Redskins (now Washington Commanders), and the Baltimore Colts (now Indianapolis Colts). The Browns won the East Division 11-1, while the Lions won the West Division 10-2. The Championship Game took place at Briggs Stadium, Detroit, on December 27th, 1953. The Lions scored first via a touchdown from HB Doak Walker (Q1: 1-yard run), and the teams exchanged field goals in the second quarter (Q2: Cle. Lou Groza 13-yard FG, Det. Doak Walker 23-yard FG). The Browns tied the game in the third quarter with a touchdown from FB Chick Jagade (Q3: 9-yard rush). The Browns then kicked two more field goals in the fourth quarter (Q4: Groza 15-yards, 43-yards) to lead 16-10. The Lions clinched the game late in the fourth when QB Bobby Lane hit WR Jim Doran in the endzone (Q4: 33-yard reception). The extra point kick from

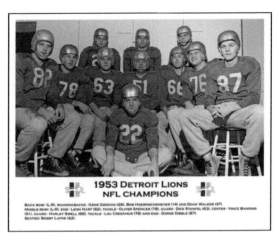

NFL Champions, Detroit Lions

Doak Walker was the game-winning point. There was no game M.V.P. in 1953.

April 4th–April 10th: National Basketball Association Finals 1953

The New York Nicks and the Minneapolis Lakers were the two teams who made the N.B.A. Finals in 1953. As with the final series for hockey and baseball, the N.B.A. finals were a best of seven series. The individual game results were:

Minneapolis Lakers, NBA champion

*04/04 NYN 96-88 ML, **04/05** NYN 71-73 ML, **04/07** ML 90-75 NYN, **04/08** ML 71-69 NYN, **04/10** ML 91-84 NYN*

George Mikan and Jim Pollard were the top scorers for the Lakers with 104 and 72 points, while on the other side of the court, Carl Braun and Connie Simmons both netted 74 points. The Lakers won the series 4-1 and there was no M.V.P.

April 9th–April 16th National Hockey League Stanley Cup 1953

The N.H.L. Stanley Cup Final in 1953 was played over seven games as it is today, and that season's title clash was between the Boston Bruins (28-29-13) and the Montreal Canadiens (28-23-19). The results for the Stanley Cup games were:

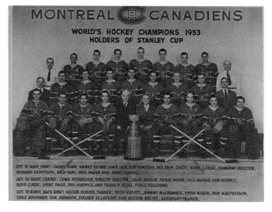

Montreal Canadiens, Stanley Cup winner

04/09 BB 2-4 MC, 04/11 BB 4-1 MC, 04/12 MC 3-0 BB, 04/14 MC 7-3 BB, 04/16 BB 0-1 MC (OT)

Maurice Richard scored 4 goals for the Canadiens, and Ken Mosdell, Calum MacKay, Dollard St. Laurent, and Doug Harvey all provided 2 assists. Ed Sandford and Milt Schmidt netted 2 goals each for the Bruins, and Fleming Mackell added 3 assists. The Montreal Canadiens won the Stanley Cup 4-1, and there was no M.V.P. Award at that time.

August 29th-September 7th: U.S. Tennis Open 1953

The men's final of the U.S. Open in 1953 was an all-American affair between Tony Trabert and Elias Victor Seixas, Jr. Trabert won in straight sets 3-0 (6-3, 6-2, 6-3). The women's final also featured two Americans, and Maureen Connolly defeated Doris Hart 2-0 (6-2, 6-4).

Connolly, who was also known as "Little Miss Mo", became the first woman to win the Grand Slam of all four major titles in a calendar year. In 1953, she beat Julia Sampson 6-3, 6-3 in the

Maureen Connolly

Australian tournament, Doris Hart 6-2, 6-3 in the French Championship, Hart again 8-6, 7-5 at Wimbledon, and finally completed the hat-trick over Hart by winning the U.S. tournament against her. Connolly claimed another record that year by becoming the only player to win all four major titles without dropping a set to an opponent.

September 30th-October 5th: Major League Baseball World Series 1953

The 1953 M.L.B. World Series was another best of seven series, and it was an entirely New York affair between the New York Yankees and the Brooklyn Dodgers. The individual game scores were:

09/30 BD 5-9 NYY, 10/01 BD 2-4 NYY, 10/02 NYN 2-3 BD, 10/03 NYY 3-7 BD, 10/04 NYN 11-7 BD, 10/05 BD 3-4 NYY

Hank Bauer, Billy Martin, and Gene Woodling scored 6, 5, and 5 runs respectively for the Yankees, and Roy Campanella, Carl Furillo, and Jim

New York Yankees versus the Brooklyn Dodgers

Gilliam hit 6, 4, and 4 runs for the Dodgers. In the pitching stakes, Allie Reynolds had 9 strikeouts for the Yankees and Carl Erskine managed 16 for the Dodgers. The New York Yankees won the World Series 4-2, and there was no M.V.P. Award during that series.

British Sports

January 10th-March 28th: Rugby Union Five Nations 1953

The 1953 Five Nations rugby union tournament was won by England. They finished top of the table with 7 points, with a record of 3 wins and 1 draw. Wales finished second on 6 points and Ireland came third with 5 points. The results for England were:

01/17 WAL 3-8 ENG, 02/14 IRE 9-9 ENG, 02/28 ENG 11-0, 03/21 ENG 26-8 SCO

Ireland v England, 1953

March 28th: Annual Oxford/Cambridge Boat Race 1953

The Oxford-Cambridge boat race on March 28th was the 99th time the two universities had competed in the historic competition. Cambridge won the race in 19 minutes 54 seconds, and won by a margin of 8 boat lengths.

Cambridge University Boat Club

May 2nd: English Division One/F.A. Cup Results 1952-1953 Season

The League Cup competition didn't start until the 1961-62 season, so the first title winners in 1953 were the Division One league winners (the top tier of English soccer now called the Premier League). The last game of the season was played on May 2nd, where Middlesbrough beat Portsmouth 4-1.

Arsenal and Preston North End both finished the season on 54 points, but Arsenal won the league with a better goal difference (33 compared to Preston's 25). Wolverhampton Wanderers were third on 51 points and West Bromwich Albion finished fourth with

League title win 1952-1953 season

50 points. The Football Association Cup was held at Wembley Stadium on the same day the league finished, May 2nd, and the match featured Blackpool against Bolton Wanderers. It was a high scoring game with goals from Nat Lofthouse (Bol.: 2 minutes), Stan Mortensen (Bpl.: 35 minutes), Willie Moir (Bol.: 39 minutes), Eric Bell (Bol.: 55 minutes), Mortensen (Blp.: 68 minutes), Mortensen (Blp. 89 minutes) and Bill Perry (Blp.: 90 minutes). Blackpool won the match 4-3.

June 22nd-July 4th: Wimbledon 1953

The Men's Wimbledon Final in 1953 was between Elias Victor Seixas, Jr. (U.S.) and Kurt Neilsen (Denmark). Seixas won the match 3 sets to love (9-1, 6-3, 6-4). The Women's Final was the second of three Grand Slam finals played that year between Maureen Connolly and Doris Hart. Connolly won the match 2 sets to love (8-6, 7-5).

Doris Hart, Shirley Fry Irvin,
and Maureen Connolly

International Sports

January 18th-September 13th: Formula 1 Motor Racing 1953

The 1953 Formula One Motor Racing Championship opened on January 18th at the Buenos Aires circuit in Argentina, and closed out with the Italian Grand Prix in Monza on September 13th. The nine-race season was won by Italian driver Alberto Ascari (Ferrari),

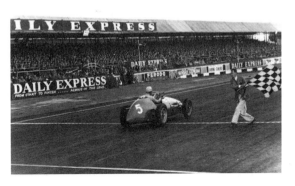

Alberto Ascari taking the chequered flag

who finished with 34.5 points. Argentina's Juan Manuel Fangio (Maserati) came second with 27.5 points. Nino Farina (Ferrari) from Italy took third place with 26 points. The Constructor Championship did not start until 1958, so there was no team award that year.

December 28th-December 31st: Davis Cup Final 1953

The 1953 Davis Cup Final was played in Melbourne, Australia, between the United States and Australia. The final round of the Davis Cup involved five matches between the two sides, and the Australians won the tournament final 3-2. The individual match results were:

Match 1 - Lew Hoad beat Elias Victor Seixas, Jr. 3-0 (6-4, 6-2, 6-3)

(From the left) Rex Hartwig, Lew Hoad, Harry Hopman, Ken Rosewall and Mervyn Rose celebrate after being presented with the Davis Cup

Match 2 - Tony Trabert beat Ken Rosewall 3-0 (6-3, 6-4, 6-4)

Match 3 - Elias Victor Seixas, Jr./Tony Trabert beat Rex Hartwig/Lew Hoad 3-0 (6-2, 6-4, 6-4)

Match 4 - Lew Hoad Beat Tony Trabert 3-2 (13-11, 6-3, 2-6, 3-6, 7-5)

Match 5 - Ken Rosewall beat Elias Victor Seixas, Jr. 3-1 (6-2, 2-6, 6-3, 6-4)

In 1953, there was no European Cup Final (it started in 1955-56), no European Cup Winners Cup (it started in 1960-61), no F.I.F.A. World Cup, no Olympic Games, no Winter Olympic Games, and no Commonwealth Games.

Chapter V: General 1953

Pop Culture

January 19th: 'I Love Lucy' Episode Watched By 71.1% Of Viewers

'I Love Lucy' was an extremely popular show during the 1950s (it ran for 180 episodes from 1951 to 1957), but on January 19th, 71.1% of American viewers/American television sets tuned in to watch the 'Lucy Goes To The Hospital' episode. This was where Lucy Ricardo (played by Lucille Ball) gave birth to Little Ricky Ricardo. Around 44 million people watched the episode. That's a staggering achievement for such an early stage of television. In modern times, the ratings are more

'I Love Lucy' cast

geared around the number of actual viewers. The highest viewing figure for a television show was the final episode of M*A*S*H on February 28, 1983, with an average of 50 million viewers (60.2%), and the most-watched broadcast ever, at present, is Super Bowl XLIX on February 1st, 2015 (where the New England Patriots beat the Seattle Seahawks 28-24), with 114.4 million viewers (47.9%) (sidmartinbio.org/vulture.com).

February 5th: Sweet Rationing Ends In United Kingdom

During World War II, a lot of things were rationed, and one of those items was sugar, which, in turn, led to the rationing of sweets. Candy, chocolate, and all sorts of things, items that children in the decades that followed would take for granted, were all strictly limited. The rationing of sweets (and many other things) began in 1940 and would continue into the fifties until February 5th when sweet rationing

On the 'Shields Daily News'

ended. There was a brief pause in the rationing of sweets during 1949, but it was reimposed due to the enormous demand. Actual sugar continued to be rationed throughout, and this ended on September 26th, 1953.

March 19th: Academy Awards First Live Broadcast

The 25th Academy Awards on March 19th were the first Oscars to be broadcast on television. The event was held at the RKO Pantages Theatre in Hollywood, hosted by Bob Hope, and it was broadcast on the N.B.C. Network. N.B.C. continued to broadcast the annual award

Bob Hope hosts the 25th Annual Academy Awards

show until 1961, when it lost out to A.B.C., which had the distinction of showing it in color for the first time in 1966. With the exception of a short period in the seventies when it returned to N.B.C., A.B.C. has shown the Oscars ever since and is contracted to continue broadcasting it until 2028.

April 13th: 'Casino Royale' Published

In April 1953, a legendary character was born, one that has long since become instantly familiar right across the world. This fictional character's name is possibly one of the most familiar of the 20th and 21st centuries. On April 15th, former British Naval Intelligence Officer, Ian Lancaster Fleming, published 'Casino Royale', the first book to feature the British spy, James Bond. It may have been the first Bond book to be written, but it was not the first Bond story to hit the big screen - that honor belonged to 'Dr. No' in 1963. There was a spoof Bond film called 'Casino Royale' starring David Niven, Peter Sellers, Woody Allen, and Ursula Andress in 1967. The story would eventually be made into a movie in 2006 when it became the 21st (presently numbering 25) official James Bond film (the first to star Daniel Craig). Both 'Casino Royale' (1967) and 'Never Say Never Again' (1983) are not considered canonical Bond films.

'Casino Royale' first edition cover

April 16th: The Launch Of Royal Yacht Britannia

The Royal Yacht Britannia was launched on April 16th from the John Brown and Company's Clydebank shipyard in Scotland. H.R.H. Queen Elizabeth II and Prince Philip, the Duke of Edinburgh, were both present for the launching ceremony,

Royal Yacht Britannia

along with a crowd of approximately 30,000. The Britannia was used by the Royal family for around 44 years and was involved in 968 official voyages across the world. She was decommissioned on December 11th, 1997, and now resides as a tourist attraction in Leith (Edinburgh).

April 24th: Winston Churchill Knighted

Sir Winston Churchill

Winston Leonard Spencer Churchill was knighted by H.R.H. Queen Elizabeth II for his contributions to the United Kingdom. He became a Knight of the Garter in recognition of his service to the country as a politician, and, as Prime Minister, leading the country during one of its darkest times (World War II).

June 30th: First Corvette Produced

The Chevrolet Corvette was first shown during the General Motors Autorama at the Waldorf Astoria in New York on January 17th. Its appearance at the show was such a success that General Motors put it into production. The first 300 Corvettes were all built at a

1953 Chevrolet Corvette

temporary factory in Flint, Michigan (315 were made during 1953), and the first production model 1953 Corvette rolled off the line on June 30th. All 300 models that were made in Flint were polo white with red interiors.

July 18th: Elvis Presley Makes First Recordings

At the age of 18, Elvis Aaron Presley recorded his first-ever song, 'My Happiness' (by The Ink Spots), at Sun Records in Memphis, Tennessee. It cost Presley $3.98 to record the two-track 78 RPM acetate record and was intended to be a gift for his mother, Gladys. He recorded a second song that day, 'That's When Your Heartaches Begin', another track from The Ink Spots. Unfortunately, Presley left the record at a friend's house when he stopped there to listen to it on the way home. The recording didn't surface

Elvis Presley

again until it was put up for auction in the 1980s, but it was never sold. It was auctioned again (along with other stuff) on the day Presley would have turned 80 and sold for $300,000 in January 2015.

September 3rd: The Establishment of the E.C.H.R.

The European Convention on Human Rights was created to protect the human rights and freedoms of every person who lived in countries that belong to the Council of Europe (a very different legal entity to The European Union). The governments that signed up to

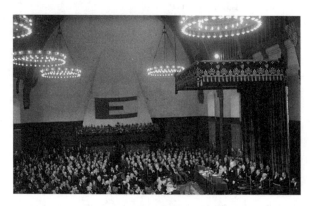

The Hall of Knights at the European Congress in The Hague

the convention legally agreed to a set of principles (18 articles) that governed behavior, protected the rule of law, promoted democracy, and defined the basic rights of people. The idea of the convention began a few years after World War II and was proposed by Winston Churchill. It was signed in 1950 and came into force on September 3rd.

November 2nd: First Call Taken By The Samaritans

For decades, the Samaritans helpline and its staff of volunteers have saved countless lives that would have otherwise been lost to suicide. The idea for the service came from one man, Reverend Chad Varah, who was the Rector at London's St. Stephen Walbrook Church. Having been moved by a teenage girl's suicide in 1935, Varah came up with the idea of the Samaritans helpline and put it into action when he was finally in a position to do so during 1953. He described the initial helpline as nothing more than "A man willing to listen, with a base and an emergency telephone."

Reverend Varah answered the very first call made to what would soon become the Samaritans on November 2nd; the phone he answered was located in the church's crypt. The name that the service would eventually employ, The Samaritans, was established about a month or so later when the Daily Mirror ran an article titled "Telephone Good Samaritans" on December 7th.

Chad Varah

December 1st: First Issue Of Playboy Is Published

Hugh Hefner, who was 27 years old in 1953, decided he wanted to publish his own magazine, and on December 1st, the very first issue of Playboy magazine hit the shelves. Hefner doubted the likely success of his new publication so much that the first issue didn't even have a date on the cover. That original issue sold for $0.50. It was the start of a magazine that went on to become a worldwide brand all of its own. That first issue is probably most remembered because it had Marilyn Monroe on the front cover and nude photos of

The first issue of Playboy magazine

the world-famous actress within its pages. Monroe never posed for Playboy, and the photos were taken four years earlier by Tom Kelley, who then sold them to a company that made calendars. Hefner eventually purchased the photos (and the rights to them) for $500 and published them in the first issue of Playboy. The issue sold over 54,000 copies, and the Playboy name went on to become a media empire.

Technological Advancements

February 28th: Double-Helix Structure of DNA Is Discovered

Rosalind Franklin in Paris

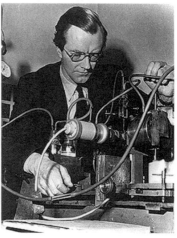
Maurice Wilkins

A monumentally important scientific breakthrough was made by American bacteriologist James D. Watson and British physicist Francis H.C. Crick in the first half of 1953. On February 28th, the pair announced they had discovered what they termed "the secret of life." The two scientists from Cambridge University had unlocked the secrets of DNA (deoxyribonucleic acid). DNA itself was discovered as far back as 1869, but it was Watson and Crick who identified the double-helix structure of DNA. Watson stated that it happened on that actual day and was not something that took days or weeks. The model of DNA that went on to become famous was completed on March 7th, and they published their results on April 25th. Watson and Crick owed some of their success to Rosalind Franklin's work, a chemist from King's College, who had used X-ray crystallography to display the helical shape that proved the models they were working on. A colleague of

James Watson and Francis Crick

Franklin, Maurice Wilkins, showed Franklin's X-ray to the two of them shortly before their discovery was made. Some reports state they give her at least a modicum of credit, but the majority have since reported that she did not get anywhere near the acknowledgment she deserved (for example, she was not included in their announcement). Either way, the double-helix discovery in February 1953 changed biology forever, and it has been instrumental in many scientific advancements that have been achieved since 1953. Both Watson and Crick (plus Wilkins) were awarded the Nobel Prize in Physiology or Medicine in 1962 for the molecular structure of DNA. Sadly, Franklin died in 1958 from cancer, and the award is not given posthumously.

May 18th: First Woman to Break the Sound Barrier

The story of Jacqueline Cochran is quite impressive. She met Floyd Bostwick Odlum, a wealthy businessman, while working at a salon in the Fifth Avenue Saks department store. Not only did he express interest in helping her to launch a cosmetic business of her own, but he was also the one who suggested she should try flying (the pair married in 1936). Cochran had been introduced to flying when she was younger and showed she was a natural by gaining her license in just three weeks. On May 18th, 1953, Cochran became the first woman to break the sound barrier. She did it flying an

Jacqueline Cochran

F-86 Sabrejet that belonged to the Royal Canadian Air Force. She took off from Edwards Air Force Base, Rogers Dry Lake, California, and during her flight reached 652.337mph. Her "wingman" on the historical flight was Major Charles "Chuck" Yeager, who was the first man to break the sound barrier in 1947. Cochran went on to become the first female pilot to break Mach 2, the first female pilot to take off from an aircraft carrier, and she broke several speed records between 1964 and 1967.

September 4th: R.E.M. Sleep Is Discovered

Eugene Aserinsky, a physiology graduate student, and Nathaniel Kleitman, Ph.D. and Chair of Physiology, published a two-page paper in a journal called Science that detailed their discovery of Rapid Eye Movement during sleep. The

Nathaniel Kleitman and Eugene Aserinsky

two of them would expand their initial report in a second published paper in 1955.

November 20th: First Man To Break Mach II

There was another major milestone in the history of flight in 1953 when pilot Albert Scott Crossfield became the first person to fly at twice the speed of sound. A familiar name to some due to his connection with "The Right Stuff" and his competitive escapades with Major Charles "Chuck" Yeager, Crossfield achieved the feat of becoming the first pilot to fly at Mach 2 in a Douglas 558-2 Skyrocket. He reached speeds of 1,291mph. However, his record lasted just a few weeks because Yeager surpassed Crossfield's record on December 12th by reaching 1,612 mph in the X-1A (historynet.com).

Albert Crossfield

Fashion

The styling of 1953 represented slender and sleek elegance, both sophisticated and young. Everything was getting shorter, from the waistlines to the hemlines, and clothing was designed for shape rather than comfort.

One of the most common accessories was gloves, and it was typical for women to wear gloves and a hat whenever they ventured out of the house. The gloves would be more formal and longer for evening wear, up to the elbows. Wide-brimmed hats were around, but the more popular were smaller

Teresita Montez in a wide-brimmed hat of Montezin straw lined in black velvet and adorned with black long-stemmed rose and black tulle by Legroux

Marilyn Monroe rocked the Cat Eye frame in 'How to Marry a Millionaire' in 1953

hats with short veils that came in a variety of colors, most notably pastel hues in the summer and spring.

Eyeglasses became more fashionable, and newer designs featured the cat's-eye style with their pointed edges and flaring. Although many opted for the black frames, colored frames were making a splash. The trend was understated and classic for jewelry, such as faux or real pearl necklaces and plastic beads. Earrings were often clip-on, and rings and watches were more subdued than flashy.

One place where comfort was starting to be taken into consideration was with women's shoes. Although high heels with a rounded toe were still favored for dressier occasions, tennis shoes and espadrilles were more fashionable for day-to-day wear.

Following women's foray into factories during WWII, they discovered the freedom of wearing trousers.

Whether they were tight-fitted or loose pants, they often had a side zipper which made them appear to be fancier than denim jeans. Capri pants were also popular, especially when partaking in outdoor activities, but for outings or

Advertising images from the 1950s

church, dresses were still the correct fashionable choice. In 1953 the hourglass figure was dominant, with waistlines cinched to accentuate the bust and hips. Corsets were common in the wardrobe, and pencil skirts were making their debut.

Prints were back after the dreariness of the War, and florals were trendy along with polka dots. Women's sleeves were often 3/4 length, and the hem of a skirt often featured an applique or embroidered design. One of the most iconic features was the felt poodle applique, particularly for rock and roll dancing evenings.

Hair was often pulled up into a ponytail, but a French twist was preferred for formal occasions. Some women opted for the 'Italian' cut, with loose curls that still looked sophisticated but had an air of freedom. Bangs were common with both long and short hairstyles and were usually relatively short but curled.

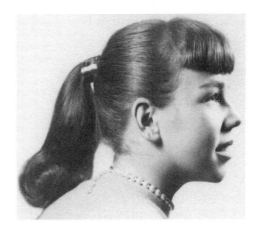

Mid-ponytail known as a horsetail

| Audrey Hepburn | Photograph of men in the 1950s wearing Bermuda shorts |

Men were starting to wear shorts more often in the 1950s, and they were typically cut and designed in the same fashion as trousers, only shorter. The shorts were pleated and came in a wide range of patterns, including checks, tartans, and plaids. College Letterman jackets were popular, as were chunky black eyeglasses frames. Men's ties were slimmer than in previous years, and many still sported a fedora hat, like Frank Sinatra.

Cars

The Hudson Hornet was the best car of 1953, with a high compression straight 6-cylinder engine that enabled the speed to reach 112 mph with proper tuning. They were certified by NASCAR and became popular on racetracks. The Hornet ranged in price from $2,543

1953 Hudson Hornet

to $3,099, and they were manufactured up until the discontinuation of the Hudson brand in mid-1957.

For luxury cars, it was hard to go past the Buick Roadmaster. The Fireball V8 engine was like nothing the public had seen before, and although it was lighter, lower, and shorter than other engines, it was more powerful by up to 11%. The car could hold six passengers, and

1953 Buick Roadmaster

there was plenty of space for luggage, even for a family going on vacation. The price of the Buick Roadmaster averaged just over $4,000.

As a modern SUV precursor, the Chevrolet Suburban was the sport utility of choice in 1953. The front bench seat was split, with two seats on the driver's side and one on the passenger side. It had a hydra-matic 4-speed automatic transmission, and some models,

1953 Chevrolet Suburban

known as Canopy express, were used for marketing or advertising. The price of these vehicles hovered around the $2,000 mark.

The top family car in 1953 was the Chevrolet Bel Air, with a cost range of $1,620 to $2,175, making it more affordable than many other vehicles at that time. The Bel Air, named after the wealthy neighborhood

1953 Chevrolet Bel Air

in Los Angeles, was designed to provide comfort. The inside and outside matched in color, and chrome details made the Bel Air an attractive vehicle that is often rebuilt nowadays as a hot rod.

The Chevrolet Corvette was the sports car of 1953, with its V8 engine and fiberglass body. There was a shortage of steel at the time, so fiberglass was the most logical choice when designing the sports car. The Corvette has inspired many songs, movies, and television shows and it is still highly sought after today. The average cost was around $3,490.

1953 Chevrolet Corvette

Production Figures in the U.S. in 1953 (www.hobbylark.com):

1. Chevrolet: 1,346,475
2. Ford: 1,247,542
3. Plymouth: 650,451
4. Buick: 488,755
5. Pontiac: 418,619
6. Oldsmobile: 334,462
7. Dodge: 320,008
8. Mercury: 305,863
9. Chrysler: 170,006
10. Studebaker: 151,576
11. DeSoto: 132,104
12. Nash: 121,793
13. Cadillac: 109,651
14. Packard: 90,252

15. Hudson: 66,143

16. Willys: 42,224

17. Lincoln: 40,762

18. Kaiser: 27,652

19. Henry J: 16,672

20. Metropolitan: 743

Popular Recreation

The most popular toy by far in 1953 was the Matchbox Cars that were sold in replica matchboxes, hence how they got their name. One of the most successful cars in the range in 1953 was the replica of Queen Elizabeth's coronation carriage. Matchbox cars were hugely popular for many decades.

1953 Vintage Matchbox Diecast Car

There were fewer cars around in 1953, so children could often be found playing in the street. Games they would play included hopscotch, ring-a-ring-a-roses, skipping rope, and hula hoops. Many didn't come home until their parents called them for dinner as it was getting dark. Collectible picture cards that came in packs of cigarettes were top-rated, especially with children, and they

An English-language Scrabble game in progress

would often trade with each other. For Christmas, the most popular gifts were the board game Scrabble and the Wiffle ball.

Television wasn't such a big deal in 1953, so most people would listen to the radio or read the newspaper. For teenagers, listening to music was their main idea of fun, and going to a dance was popular, often with a chaperone or very strict rules from their parents. Interestingly, these dances were often called 'sock hops' because they had to take their shoes off, so the floor didn't get damaged!

Ice cream parlors, pizza parlors, and malt shops were all popular gathering places for teens and adults. The drive-in movies or the theater were other popular pastimes in the evening. The drive-ins were an excellent economical choice because you could get several people in each car and only pay the one price. Food and drinks could be purchased there, and it was also a popular place to take a date.

Yum Eurich's Old Fashioned Ice Cream Parlor

There was a significant emphasis on family entertainment in 1953, and parents typically engaged in activities with their children. They would hop into the family car and go for a drive around town on Sundays or go for picnics at the beach or the park. Many families would play board games or card games at night.

At work in an ice cream parlor in 1950

Sport was popular, especially football, baseball, and basketball, and fans could go and watch the games being played live. Others who were lucky enough to have a television could watch sports being broadcast. Golfing was becoming a trendy sport, and bowling was both a family activity and one where friends could hang out and have a game. Going boating was a popular recreational activity, so if you owned a boat, you generally had lots of friends! When thinking about recreational activities in the 1950s, they can generally be described as good, clean, fun. Children were able to amuse themselves outside in the sunshine and could do so reasonably safely. It was very family-oriented, and those allowed out to the dances knew there would be dire consequences if they broke the rules.

Orange County Coast Association golfers

Bowling club at Holtenauer Strasse 279

Boating in the 1950s

Chapter VI: Births & Deaths 1953

Births (onthisday.com)

January 5th - Pamela Sue Martin: American Actress

January 6th - Malcolm Young: Australian Guitarist

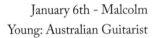

January 10th - Pat Benatar: American Singer and Songwriter

January 15th - Randy White: American N.F.L. Football Player

January 23rd - Robin Zander: American Vocalist and Guitarist

January 24th - Nigel Glockler: English Drummer

January 25th - The Honky Tonk Man/Wayne Farris: American Wrestler

February 16th - André St. Laurent: Canadian N.H.L. Ice Hockey Player

February 18th - Robin "Robbie" Bachman: Canadian Drummer

February 21st - William Petersen: American Actor

February 26th - Michael Bolton: American Singer and Songwriter

March 7th - Kenny Aronoff: American Drummer

March 13th - Andy Bean: American Golfer

March 24th - Louie Anderson: American Comedian

April 18th - Rick Moranis: Canadian Actor

April 27th - Ellen S. Baker: American Physician and NASA Astronaut

May 6th - Tony Blair: British Prime Minister of the U. K.

May 8th - Alex Van Halen: American Drummer

May 15th - George Brett: American M.L.B. Baseball Player

May 15th - Mike Oldfield: British Musician

May 16th - Pierce Brosnan: Irish Actor

May 16th - Rick Rhoden: American M.L.B. Baseball Player

May 29th - Danny Elfman: American Film Composer, Singer, and Songwriter

June 2nd - Craig Stadler: American Golfer

June 13th - Tim Allen: Canadian Comedian and Actor

June 15th - Xi Jinping: Chinese President

June 22nd - Cyndi Lauper: American Singer, Songwriter and Actress

June 29th - Don Dokken: American Singer and Musician

July 11th - Leon Spinks: American Boxer

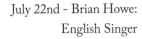

July 22nd - Brian Howe: English Singer

July 23rd - Graham Gooch: English Cricket Player

August 1st - Robert Cray: American Singer and Guitarist

August 8th - Nigel Mansell: British Racing Driver

August 11th - Hulk Hogan/Terry Bollea: American Wrestler

August 14th - James Horner: American Composer

August 16th - Kathie Lee Gifford: American Television Presenter, Singer, and Actress

August 30th - Robert Parish: American N.B.A. Basketball Player

September 11th - Tommy Shaw: American Guitarist, Singer, and Songwriter

October 7th - Hector "Tico"Torres: American Drummer, Percussionist and Songwriter

October 15th - Tito Jackson: American Singer

October 27th - Michael Baker: American U.S.N. Lt. Commander and NASA Astronaut

November 1st - Jan Davis: American Astronaut

November 13th - Tracy Scoggins: American Actress

December 8th - Kim Basinger: American Actress

December 9th - John Malkovich: American Actor

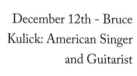

December 12th - Bruce Kulick: American Singer and Guitarist

December 13th - Ben Bernanke: American Economist

December 17th - Bill Pullman: American Actor

Deaths (onthisday.com)

January 1st - Hank Williams: American Singer, Songwriter and Musician

January 2nd - Guccio Gucci: Italian Businessman and Fashion Designer

January 24th - Ben Taylor: American Baseball Player and Manager

March 5th - Joseph Stalin: Soviet Union Leader

March 28th - Jim Thorpe: American Athlete and Olympic gold medalist

May 27th - Jesse Burkett: American M.L.B. Baseball Player

June 5th - Bill Tilden: American Tennis Player

August 11th - Tazio Nuvolari: Italian Racing Driver

August 22nd - Jim Tabor: American M.L.B. Baseball Player

September 5th - Francis Ford: American Actor film actor, writer and director

September 28th - Edwin Hubble: American Astronomer

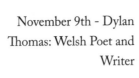

November 9th - Dylan Thomas: Welsh Poet and Writer

December 2nd - Ernie Hayes: English Cricketer

December 19th - Robert A. Millikan: American Experimental Physicist, Nobel Prize in Physics (1923)

Chapter VII: Statistics 1953

* U.S. GDP 1953 - 389.2 Million US$ (countryeconomy.com)

* U.S. GDP 2020 - 20.953 Trillion US$ (worldbank.org)

* U.K. GDP 1957 - 61.96 Million US$ (countryeconomy.com)

* U.K. GDP 2020 - 2.76 Trillion US$ (worldbank.org)

* U.S. Inflation (% Change in C.P.I.) 1960 - 1.5% (globaleconomy.com)

* U.S. Inflation (% Change in C.P.I.) 2020 - 1.2% (globaleconomy.com)

* U.K. Inflation (% Change in C.P.I.) 1960 - 1% (globaleconomy.com)

* U.K. Inflation (% Change in C.P.I.) 2020 - 1% (globaleconomy.com)

* U.S. Population 1953 - 165,909,996 (populationpyramid.net)

* U.S. Population 2020 - 329,484, 123 (worldbank.org)

* U.K. Population 1953 - 50,750,980 (populationpyramid.net)

* U.K. Population 2020 - 67,215,293 (worldbank.org)

* U.S. Population By Gender 1953 - F: 83,375,617 M: 82,534,379 (populationpyramid.net)

* U.S. Population By Gender 2020 - F: 166,449,500 M: 163,034,623 (worldbank.org)

* U.K. Population By Gender 1953 - F: 26,357,087 M: 24,393,893 (populationpyramid.net)

* U.K. Population By Gender 2020 - F: 34,004, 276 M: 33,211,017 (worldbank.org)

* U.S. Life Expectancy At Birth 1953 - 68.71 (macrotrends.net)

* U.S. Life Expectancy At Birth 2020 - 78.852 (worldbank.org)

* U.K. Life Expectancy At Birth 1953 - 69.41 (macrotrends.net)

* U.K. Life Expectancy At Birth 2020 - 81.371 (worldbank.org)

* U.S. Annual Working Hours Per Worker 1953 - 2,020 (ourworldindata.org)

* U.S. Annual Working Hours Per Worker 2017 - 1,757 (ourworldindata.org)

* U.K. Annual Working Hours Per Worker 1953 - 2,165 (ourworldindata.org)

* U.K. Annual Working Hours Per Worker 2017 - 1,670 (ourworldindata.org)

* U.S. Unemployment Rate 1953 - 2.9 (stlouisfed.org)

* U.S. Unemployment Rate 2019 - 3.788 (index.mundi.com)

* U.K. Unemployment Rate 1953 - 2.03 (stlouisfed.org)

* U.K. Unemployment Rate 2019 - 4.229 (index.mundi.com)

* U.S. Prison Population 1950 - 264,620 (prisonstudies.org)

* U.S. Prison Population 2018 - 2,102,400 (prisonstudies.org)

* U.K. Prison Population 1955 - 21,134 (prisonstudies.org)

* U.K. Prison Population 2020 - 79,514 (prisonstudies.org)

* U.S. Cost Of Living - $100 in 1953 would equate to the spending power of $1,062.61 in 2022. That is a total change of 962.61% in around seventy years (in2013dollars.com).

* U.K. Cost Of Living - £100 in 1953 would equate to the spending power of £2,975.00 in 2022. That is a total change of 2,875.00% in around seventy years (in2013dollars.com).

Cost Of Things

In 1953, the cost of various things, be it a house or a loaf of bread, was considerably different to what people would pay in 2023. Here are some of the prices charged for various items in 1953:

United States

* One Dozen Eggs - $0.70 (stacker.com)
* One Pound Of White Bread - $0.16 (stacker.com)
* Half-Gallon Of Fresh Milk - $0.47 (stacker.com)
* Average Salary Per Person - $4,200 (census.gov)
* Average Cost Of A House - $9,550 (doyouremember.com)
* Average Price Of A Car - $3,490 (cheapism.com)
* Average Price Of A Gallon Of Petrol - $0.29 (titlemax.com)

United Kingdom (Based On 1955 Prices)

* Half-Dozen Eggs - £0.08 (mirror.co.uk)
* Loaf Of White Bread - £0.04 (mirror.co.uk)
* Pink Of Milk - £0.03 (mirror.co.uk)

* Average Salary Per Person (1957) - £7.50 Per Week/£390 Per Year (express.co.uk)

* Average Cost Of A House - £1,891 (sunlife.co.uk)

* Price Of A Car (Ford Popular)- £391 (motoringresearch.com)

* Average Price Of A Gallon Of Petrol - £0.22 (mirror.co.uk)

Chapter VIII: Iconic Advertisements of 1953

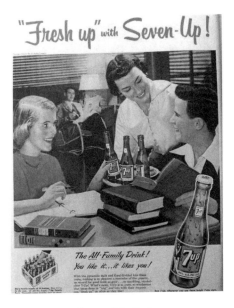

Seven-Up Soda

Lucky Strike

Quaker Oats

Dodge, 'The Action Car for Active Americans'

Marmite

Dickies

Squirt

U.S. Howland Hair Dry Swim Caps

Philip Morris

Alcoa Aluminum

Schick 20

Coca-Cola

Mercury

Chesterfield

Palmolive Brilliantine

Northwest Airlines

Tide

Eno

Kodak

General Electric

Listerine Antiseptic

Lustre-Creme Shampoo

Gem Razor

I have a gift for you!

Dear reader, thank you so much for reading my book!

To make this book more (much more!) affordable, the images are all black & white, but I've created a special gift for you!

You can now have access, for FREE, to the PDF version of this book with the original images!

Keep in mind that some are originally black & white, but a lot of them are colored.

I hope you enjoy it!

Download it here:

http://bit.ly/3Avd5cJ

Or Scan this QR Code:

I have a favor to ask you!

I deeply hope you've enjoyed reading this book and felt transported right into 1953!

I loved researching it, organizing it, and writing it, knowing that it would make your day a little brighter.

If you've enjoyed it too, I would be extremely grateful if you took just a few minutes to leave a positive customer review and share it with your friends.

As an unknown author, that makes all the difference and gives me the extra energy I need to keep researching, writing, and bringing joy to all my readers. Thank you!

Best regards,
Edward L. Jones

Please leave a positive book review here:

http://amzn.to/3hMvTxG

Or Scan this QR Code:

Check Our Other Books!

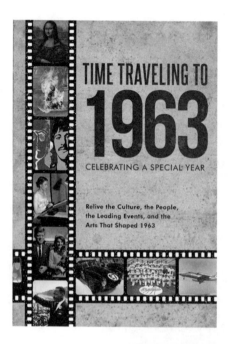